Tihar Festival in Nepal (Diwali)

Important Events in Tihar

Asmita Jha

pencil

ISBN 978-93-5667-340-3
© Asmita Jha 2022
Published in India 2022 by Pencil

A brand of

One Point Six Technologies Pvt. Ltd.
123, Building J2, Shram Seva Premises,
Wadala Truck Terminal, Wadala (E)
Mumbai 400037, Maharashtra, INDIA
E connect@thepencilapp.com
W www.thepencilapp.com

Author biography

I, Asmita Jha loves writing articles related to culture. I love those traditions which are filled with joy and entertainment. I know that these festivals are celebrated with certain reasons. Also, in such festivals, people get to spend enough time with their friends and family members. As our life has become very busy, festivals are the greatest ways to overcome our tiredness.

CONTENTS

Deusi-Bhailo

Deusi-Bhailo

-A famous game played by the Nepalese during Tihar.

-A team of 5-10 people (children as well as adults) is made.

-The children are excited for this one month before Tihar.

-In school too, they spend most of the time planning for this event.

-The teams dance and sing by going to various people's homes.

-They sing deusi-bhailo songs.

-Some also use musical instruments like guitars and dhol for making the event filled with more pleasure.

-The guardian of the house distributes sel roti (a ring-like bread), anarsa (a sweet bread), and other food items along with some money.

-The team members then distribute the money and offerings among themselves.

-Bhailo song is generally sung by girls and Deusi boys.

-The girls who play bhailo are called 'Bhailini' and the boys who play Deusi are called 'Deuse'.

-It is played from the day of Laxmi Puja to Bhaitika.

-The offerings given during Deusi-Bhailo are also called 'Kartik dan'.

-Programs are also organized by 'Myadi Prahari' (periodic police) teams in Panchthar.

History

-Previously, these games were not played in Kathmandu, Lalitpur, and Bhaktapur.

-Generally played in village areas.

-Rather, the teams used to ask for Yomari during Yomari Purnima (a festival of the Newar community).

Some Deusi-Bhailo Songs

'Ae Bhana Bhana Bhai Ho
Deusi Re
Ae Ramrari Bhana
Deusi Re
Ae Swar Milai Kana
Deusi Re
Ae Bhana na Bhana
Deusi Re
Ae Rato Mato
Deusi Re
Ae Chiplo Bato
Deusi Re
Ae Laddai Paddai
Deusi RE
Ae Ayeka Hami
Deusi Re
Ae Plastic ko Goli
Deusi Re
Ae Bhai Tika Voli
Deusi Re
Ae Kera ko Khamba
Deusi Re
Ae Dus Bhai Jamma
Deusi Re
Ae Hami Tesai

Deusi Re
Ae ayeka hoinau
Deusi Re
Ae Bali Raja Le
Deusi Re
Ae Pathayeka
Deusi Re
Ae Cycle ko Ghanti
Deusi Re
Ae Chhito Garnus Aunty
Deusi Re
Ae Akhum Bakhum
Deusi Re
Ae Sel Roti Chakhum
Deusi Re
Ae Chhana Mathi Aduwa
Deusi Re
Ae Hamra Sathi Paduwa
Deusi Re
Ae Chhana Mathi Ghiraula
Deusi Re
Ae K K Dinxan Heraula
Deusi Re..........'

Meaning: 'We, 10 friends, have come saying 'Deusi Re' through a slippery road by facing many difficulties. We have come to see what we are given. We also need to go to other houses. Please do it fast. We want to taste your selroti.....'

'Jhilimili Raat Ma
Sathi Vai Sathma
Ramailo Manaudai
Laddai Ra Paddai

Ayeka Hami

Deusi Re Vatyaudai…'

Meaning: 'We all friends have come on this twinkling night. We have managed to come on this slippery road, by enjoying the whole route, playing 'Deusi'……..'.

Deusi-Bhailo for Limbus

-Limbus blow 'chyabrung baja' (a kind of musical instrument) and play deusi in Taplenjung. This instrument is also known as 'Balihang Tamanag'.

-Limbus also called Deusi-Bhailo a 'Laringen' and 'Namlingen'.

-They sing in chorus.

-On this day, Limbus wear various pieces of jewellery and cultural dress to show their culture. They spend some money earned from Deusi-Bahailo for the protection of their culture and social works.

-Story:

-It is said that the last king of Limbus 'Balihang' requested his country people to be awake the whole night and perform dancing as well as singing to wish for his longer life.

Important Things in Tihar

Rangoli

-Also called as 'Alpana'.

-Came from the word 'Rangawali' meaning 'queue of colours'.

-Made in Tihar as well as other Yagyas & Hawans (worships done to eliminate bad omens), and Worships.

-A sign of positive energy before starting any good work (suvakarya).

-A traditional skill 'lokkala'.

-One of the 64 skills mentioned in the 'Kamsutra of Watsyayan', a holy book.

-Is a sign of cultural, spiritual, and religious beliefs.

-Importance: Purification of House, Spreading of Positive Energy, Elimination of Negative Energy

-A symbolic shape

-Best Direction for making rangoli is n front of the Main Gate of the House for welcoming the Goddess.

-First, the house is cleaned and painted for purification and then rangoli is drawn.

Different kinds of Rangoli Designs

Traditional Rangoli

-Shape of 'Swastik' sign (a sign indicating well-being) or 'Lord Ganesh' is drawn.

-Has some simple geometrical shapes and pictures of various gods and goddesses are drawn.

-Various colours or 'sindur' (a holy color put by hindu married women on their forehead) is used.

-Even dry powders can be utilized.

-Rice is wetted in various colours the night before.

-White colour: Rice flour or white chalk powder.

-Has lines and dots in this design.

Amurta Rangoli

-Use of glitter.

-A large flower is put in the centres and shining colours are put around it.

God Rangoli

-Pictures of gods and goddesses are drawn here.

-Generally, Lord Ganesh's shape is made but it's not a rule.

-People can draw any god or goddess's picture based on his/her desire.

Flower Rangoli

-Use of Sayapatri (marigold) and 'Makhamali' flowers (purple colorrd small ball like flowers which never dry).

Geometric Rangoli

-Lines and various geometric designs are made.

-Diyo can also be used.

Diyo (Traditional oil Lamps), the Main Decoration of Tihar

-These are the main decorations of Tihar.

-Diyo generally refers to a small bowl-shaped piece of clay.

-In it, people put a line-like structure made of cotton.

-That structure is dipped in oil.

-Then, it is burnt and put in diyo.

-That diyo along with batti is known as 'diyo-batti'.

-They are kept in houses so that there is light during darkness.

-In clay diyos, oil was put and a cotton batti was kept inside it and lit with matches.

-During Tihar, this diyos were put in every corner of the house to emit light ('jhilimili').

Roti

Selroti: Ring-like breads.

Finiroti: a special bread dipped in 'chasni' (boiled sugar solution)

Arsa Roti: sweet bread made from jaggery and rice flour.

Tharu Roti: A kind of sweet bread made by Tharu

Jhiniya Roti: Chips like bread

References

दियो बाली साँझको… – Online Khabar

https://geetsangeetnepal.com/hurra-dance-as-the-identity-of-the-magar-caste/

'काठमाडौंमा देउसी-भैलो गाउँबाट भित्रिएको हो'- विविधा - कान्तिपुर समाचार (ekantipur.com)

मनाइयो कुकुर तिहार- समाचार - कान्तिपुर समाचार (ekantipur.com)

न्हू दँया भिन्तुना- फोटोफिचर - कान्तिपुर समाचार (ekantipur.com)

जनकपुरमा छठको तयारी पूरा – Online Khabar
https://www.jagranjosh.com/general-knowledge/chhath-puja-10-amazing-facts-about-history-origin-and-rituals-1478176414-1

हराउँदै 'सोरठी नाच' – Online Khabar

https://en.wikipedia.org/wiki/Sama_Chakeva
https://nepaltraveller.com/sidetrack/sama-chakeva

Precautions During Tihar

-In wooden houses, the diyos may cause a fire.

-Child care should be given priority to care for them during the fire.

-Beware of short circuits.

-Water should be available so that if accidentally fire occurs, it can be extinguished.

-Blowing of 'Patakas' (those which create noise and fire) should be banned.

The 5 Days of Tihar

Days of Tihar1

Days	Worship of
Kartik Krishna Dwadashi	Elephant and Lord Ganesh
Kartik Krishna Trayodashi	Crow
Kartik Krishna Chaturdashi	Dog
Kartik Aunshi	Cow and Goddess Laxmi
Kartik Shukla Pratipada	Gobardhan and Bali
Kartik Shukla Dwitiya	Brothers

Day	Festival
1	Kag Tihar (Worship of Crows)
2	Kukur Tihar (Worship of Dogs)
3	Laxmi Puja/ Gai Tihar (Worship of Goddess Laxmi

	and Cows)
4	Gobardhan Puja/ Mhapuja/ Goru Tihar/ Balipuja (Worship of Oxen, Mhapuja: Self-Worship done by Nepal Community, Nepal Sambat, the Newari New Year is also celebrated on this day)
5	Vaitika/Kijapuja (Worship of Brother by Sisters)

History of Tihar

-72 years ago, during the Rana regime, 'Tihar' was celebrated only on the basis of an order given by 'Shree 3 Maharaj', the Rana prime minister.

-In Kathmandu, Lalitpur, and Bhaktapur, jhyali (trumpet-a Nepali musical instrument used to play classical and folk songs) was beaten and 'juwa' (the gambling game) was played. This event was also known as 'Jhyali pitera juwa fukaune kaam'.

-If they played gambling (juwa) without the prime minister's order, they were punished.

-People used to say in jhyali 'Maharaj ko hukum le aja dekhi juwa fukyo' which meant that we have started playing gambling as per the order of our respected prime minister.

-Teams were made to play gambling around Mangalbazar of Patan and Taumadi of Bhaktapur.

-After the completion of the Rana regime, gambling was ended by making various laws.

Kag Tihar

Kag Tihar/Dhanteras/Dhan Trayodashi
Kag Puja
-Falls on the day of Trayodashi.

-On that day, the children call the crows from the morning.

-Even those people generally curse the crows as 'Chandaal' for throwing off the pot of 'Amrit' (the drink which could cancel the death of people) worship the crows and provide food.

-Crows are traditionally considered as 'Yamadut' (an agent of 'Yama', the god of death) or 'Sandesbahak'.

-It is believed that if some eats without worshipping the crows on this day, they can have to go to hell.

Dhanteras/ Dhan Trayodashi
-It is believed that 'Dhanwantari' was incarnated on this day.

-Hence, mainly 'Vaidyaraj' (a kind of doctor) was worshipped as 'Dhanwantari' on this day.

-Most people buy utensils and use them on this day.

-Some people even buy new pieces of jewellery on this day.

-This day is preferred for buying and using these new pieces of jewellery and utensils to bring richness, prosperity, and happiness.

Kukur Tihar

Kukur Tihar and Narak Chaturdashi
Kukur Tihar
-Third day of Tihar.
-Celebrated on Kartik Krishna Chaturdashi.
-Dog, (Kukur), the baahan (animals on which gods ride while going anywhere) of god 'Dharmaraj' is worshipped by offering delicious food and worshipping them.
-Dog is generally considered as 'baahan' of God 'Bhairab' or 'Yamadut'.
-Story: The guards of Yamaraj are the dogs named 'Shyam' and 'Sabal' who show the roads when dead people reach Yamalok. (The place where Yamaraj, the god of death, lives).
- Yamalok is the place where Yamaraj, the god of death, lives.

Celebration of Kukur Puja by Nepal Police
-'Dogs Training Centre' working under Nepal Police also performs worshipping of dogs on this day.
-Dogs are seen to aid in various ways during research done by police like finding bombs, addictive items, and tracking research.
-Some dogs are allowed to play various kinds of games on this day.
-8 types of dogs are trained by the police in Nepal.

Narak Chaturdashi

-It is also celebrated on this day. For celebrating this festival, in the morning, people go to various rivers or lakes, take bath, do 'tarpan' (worship of ancestors), and light 'Yamadip' (a small lamp used for worshipping God Yama) with a belief that they don't have to go to 'narak' (hell) after death.

Importance of Dog

-A domestic animal

-A faithful animal.

-Protects from theft and robbery.

-Helps police in identifying thieves and doubtful things.

-Aids the shepherds in protecting sheep, and goats from the wind animals.

Laxmi Puja or Gai Tihar

Laxmi Puja

-3rd day of Tihar

-Goddess Laxmi is worshipped on this day.

-She is the goddess of richness and happiness.

-Diyo is a sign of brightness

-Old concept: when lighting the diyo, there comes peace, happiness, and energy. Thus, tihar is also known as the festival of dipawali.

-Is formed from 2 words:- 'Deep': diyo and 'awali': in line. Thus, the word 'Deepawali' means diyo enlightened in line.

-All parts of the house are cleaned and decorated.

-In the evening, worship is done by lighting diyos and incense sticks by offering money, rice, paddy, fruits, pieces of bread, garlands, and delicious foods to welcome and impress her.

-Mainly, the painted picture of Goddess Laxmi in paper or her statue is worshipped.

-Also, 'Dhanadev'/Kuber, the 'digpal' of the north direction among 8 digpals (nickname for different directions) is worshiped on this day.

-Moreover, the daughters are worshipped as well considering them as the incarnation of Goddess Laxmi.

-Deusi-Bhailo is also played by children.

-The offerings are eaten and used as 'Prasad' after the

completion of worship.

Method of Worship As Mentioned in Holy Books

-After cleaning the house, the cow should be worshipped in the morning.

-In the evening, 'Deepawali' is done by lighting diyos, candles, and twinkling bulbs.

-A mandap (temporary platform made for welcoming goddess Laxmi) is made along with the mandap of flowers and oil

-Curd, banana, raddish, fruits, pieces of bread, etc. are then offered.

-After that, the goddess is worshipped.

-While worshipping, the person should imagine the goddess as dressed in a yellow dress with various pieces of jewellery, curly hair, a smiling face, and sitting on the tortoise.

-Then, food and money are offered.

-Following that, the offered Prasad and flowers are distributed to all the family members.

Stories Behind Laxmi Puja

-In Tretayug: Shriram, Laxman, and Sita completed 14 years of banwas and returned home. On the day of Karti Krishna paksha-ausi, there was darkness. so, on this dark night, the diyos were enlightened in line to welcome them. From that time, this ritual of enlightening diyo is called as 'Deepawali'.

-This day was separated for the worship of Goddess Laxmi. Thus, various gods and goddesses celebrated it with happiness.

-Also, it is believed that on this day, King Bali got back his kingdom, thus this day is celebrated as the day of richness.

-On this day, Lord Bishnu killed the devil 'Narakashur' and peace was obtained.

-On this day, King Ram became the king of Ayodhya.

-The new year of 'Arya' culture (the culture of King Ram) is celebrated.

Religious Beliefs Behind Tihar

-Belief 1:

It is believed that, on the night of Laxmi Puja, goddess Laxmi moves around the whole world. Goddess Laxmi is impressed by the brightness of diyos at home. And due to this, happiness, and peace comes inside the home.

-Diyos are enlightened at worshipping place, main gate and other parts of the house in the name of kuldevta (main god) and other gods and goddesses.

-Almost all parts of the house like rooms, gates, windows, ladders, etc. are cleaned on this day.

-Belief 2:

-Goddess Laxmi doesn't prefer darkness. She lives only in those clean and bright houses.-Thus, people paint and beautify their houses to welcome her and light clay-Diyos at every place in the house.

Gobardhan Puja

Gobardhan Puja/ Mhapuja/ Goru Tihar/ Balipuja
Introduction

-As 'oxen' called 'goru' in Nepal are worshipped on this day, the day is known as 'Goru Puja'.

-Also, the worship of Gobardhan Mountain is performed on the same day, hence the day being called as 'Gobardhan Puja' too.

-Mhapuja is also a name for this day on which self-Worship done by Nepal Community. which is the self-worship done by Newars with the belief that 'if we can make ourselves satisfied and happy, we can please the god and receive blessings, as well as our life, can be meaningful.' Mha Puja is also done with the aim of body purification.

-Moreover, 'Nepal Sambat', the Newari New Year is celebrated on this day. To celebrated this, rallies are organized by the Newari people saying 'Nyudaya Vintuna' which means 'happy new year' in Kathmandu, Lalitpur, Bhaktapur, Banepa, Dhulikhel, Barhabise, and Dolakha. Not only this, such rallies are conducted in Hetauda as well with various Newari musical instruments. In Kathmandu, they generally move around Basantapur palace by performing several Newari dances and blowing musical instruments.

History Behind Nepal Sambat

-The Nepal Sambat was started by Shankhadhar Sakhwa. This Sambat was utilized as Maulik (fundamental) sambat in Nepal till the ruling period of of King Prithvi Narayan Shah. Nepal Sambat is named so because it follows the name of this country. Before the Lichhavi period, Shak sambat was used. After the introduction of democracy in 2007, Nepal Sambat is given national value. On this day (aunsi), the 'bahi khata' (previous years acoount) is closed and on the next day (pratipada), a new 'bahi khata' is opened.

Stories for the Day of Gobardhan Puja

Story 1:

In Dwapar yuga, the inhabitants of Gokul used to worship Lord Indra. But Lord Krishna told them to stop worshipping God Indra and convinced them to worship Gobardhan Parwat. Due to this, Lord Indra became angry and thus generated a dangerous rainfall. To protect the people, Lord Krishna lifted Gobardhan Parwat on his hands so that the rain would not affect anyone. This destroyed the boasting attitude of Lord Indra and hence he came to visit Lord Krishna. From that day, Gobardhan Parwat is worshipped on the day of Gobardhan Puja.

Story 2:

King Bali had imprisoned Goddess Laxmi. So, he was very rich. But he had a quality that he donated anything desired by any person who came to him. One day, Lord Narayan took the form of Brahman (Baman) and came to visit his palace. He took a huge shape and put one leg in the sky and another leg on the earth touching the head of king Bali. Due to this, King Bali reached Patal Lok (a part of the universe) and obtained the kingdom there. After that, Goddess Laxmi was made free. Thus, this day is celebrated to express gratefulness to king Bali for having carried a load of earth at that time.

How is Mha Puja Celebrated---

-On the day of Kartik Shukla Pratipada on which the moon shines and pratipada occurs for only a little time, people perform worship on this day with various rituals. They take bath by facing the moon, then wear pure clothes, donate something they can, and worship the gods 'Gobardhan' as well as King Bali. They also worship the moon after these rituals. Then, they make a mandap and surround it with paddy, lawa (puffed paddy), and Akshata (holy rice), collectively called as 'Aankhe'. In the Mandap, they also put the broom, earthen pot (ghaito), nanglo (round woven bamboo tray), etc. In front of the mandap, they put 'Bimiro' (a lemon-like citrus fruit), Banana, Walnut, and other fruits. Also, they decorate it with makhamali flowers and a rope of thread. Then, they worship their body by moving the earthen pot (called 'ghat') and broom (jhadu) up and down. After that, they take curd and 'sang' (a combination of all the things during Mha puja) which is done for good luck. It is believed that if the 'sang' is taken without facing the moon, bad luck may happen. Thus, they should be on the right of the moon or in its front while taking 'sang'. Thus, as soon as the moon shines on this day, Nepal Sambat is renewed. Following that, they eat their favourite food and put the pan (a kind of leaf with a good smell') and supari ('beetle nut') in their mouth for purification. They don't sleep on the night of Mha puja. Instead, they should play some game in which there is the sound of money. It is believed that if anyone wins the game, his/her whole year is filled with happiness and prosperity.

Story Behind Mha Puja

Story of Mha Puja

-1089 years ago, an inhabitant of Kathmandu, Shankhadahar Sakhuwa paid the loan of every Nepali at that time. Thus, Nepal Sambat was introduced to remember the freedom of Nepali from debt. There is an interesting story about how he collected so much money to pay the debt of everyone. It is believed that t that time, once, a 'Jyotishi' set a specific time 'sait' of taking sand in 'Laghutirtha', the middle of Bishnumati and Bhadramati rivers and sending it to Kathmandu. Sankhadhar Sakhuwa bought that sand for his own work. Actually, the holy sand was to be turned into gold. But the people who were carrying the sand thought it as an ordinary one and sold it. Instead, they took another ordinary sand and submitted it to Jyotishi. As the sand was not taken at a specific time (sait), it didn't turn into gold. However, the one bought by Sankhadhar turned into gold. He became very happy. But being religious and kind, he decided to use that gold for a strong purpose. Thus, he took permission from King Jayadev and paid the debt of every Nepali. After that, the pressure of celebrating 'Shak sambat' and 'Thakuri Sambat' which were related to discrimination was eliminated. Thus, Mha Puja is celebrated on this day.

Bhai Tika or Kijapuja

Introduction

-Also called 'Yamadwitiya'.

-In the Newari language, this day is known as 'Kijapuja'.

-Falls on Kartik Shukla Dwitiya.

-Balgopaleshwor mandir, a temple in the middle of Ranipokhari of Kathmandu, is opened on this day.

-In this temple, those who don't have brother or sister come, worship the idol of god 'Gopal' (another name for Lord Krishna) present in the temple and put tika from the hands of priests.

-Also, Khanjaneshwor Mahadev Temple present at Jayabageshwari of the Pashupati area is open only on this day for such people.

Histoy of opening the 2 temples on Vaitika

--Before 2035, only Khanjaneshwor temple was opened on this day. Balgopaleshwor temple was closed as the people used to jump in the water of Ranipokhari for entry. After 2035, this temple was also opened. However, the earthquake of 2072 destroyed this temple. So, only Khanjaneshwor temple was opened on this day. Now, from 2077, Balgopaleshwor temple again came into existence.

Events in Bhai Tika

-Sisters worship the Astadal kept in the main plate after worshipping Lord Ganesh, the Kalash, and Diyos.

-The Astadal indicates Markendeya, Bali, Aswatthama, Vyas, Kripacharya, Bibhishan, Hanuman, and Parshuram. They indicate asta Chiranjeevi, Chitragupta, yamaraj, Yamuna, Dharmaraj, and Ganapatya.

-They put their brothers inside a mandap bounded by oil and put a seven-coloured or five-coloured tika with garlands of different flowers like makhamali, sayapatri, and Godavari.

-Sisters put tika (Saptarangi-7 colours or Pancha Rangi-5 colours) on their brothers' foreheads and wish for their longer life, prosperity, and happiness.

-The 5 main colours used in the tika are red, white, yellow, green, and blue.

-They also put the garland of the 'makhamali' (maranth, an unfading kind of flower) flower on their brother's neck so that as long as the garland doesn't dry, Yamaraj can't take their brother's life.

-Also, they make the mandap of oil so that their brother can be alive as long as it is not dried.

-Morever, they put the walnut in water so that as long as the walnut doesn't sink in water, their brother is alive.

-After that, the brothers also put tika on their sisters' foreheads.

-The sisters consider their elder brother as 'Yamaraj' and younger brother as 'Chitragupt' and thus worship them by making mandap.

-After the worship is completed, they present their brothers with the food cooked by them followed by pan (betel leaves) and supari (betle nut) for making their mouths pure.

-It is believed that the worship done by the sisters helps to bring success and richness and prosperity in their brothers' life.

-After putting tika, sisters give okhar (walnut), katus, sel roti, and spices (mainly dry fruits, lwang {cloves}, sukumel {cardamom), etc.).

-Following that, the brothers provide gifts as desired by their sisters. The gifts include clothes, money, or other items.

Stories Behind Bhai Tika

Story 1:

On the day of Kartik Shukla Dwitiya, Yamuna ji invited her brother 'Yamaraj' and presented him with food with proper worship as demanded. At that time, Yamuna ji asked for a blessing from her brother 'those sisters and brothers who perform worship on this day should be happy and rich'. Yamaraj accepted this and blessed her. From that day, this day is celebrated as 'Vratridwitiya'.

Story 2:

Once upon a time, Yamaraj was coming to take a dead person with Yamaduts. The sister of that dead person asked Yamaraj for the permission to perform vaitika by requesting 'Can you please wait till I perform Vaitika'. Yamaraj agreed. Yamaraj agreed as on that day, the 'Vaitika' celebration was going on. Thus, she worshipped her brother and also performed the worship of Yamaraj and Yamaduts. After that, she asked for her brother's life by applying a trick. She requested to god Yamaraj 'please don't take my brother till the oil mandap doesn't dry, the walnut doesn't sink in water, and the makhamali garland doesn't dry'. Yamaraj was impressed with the sister's intelligence and agreed. Thus, the person's life was saved as the makhamali flower and never dry and the walnut never sinks in water.

Chhath Puja

Introduction

-Generally celebrated by Bhojpuri and Maithili communities.

-It is celebrated in the belief of fighting various kinds of diseases.

-Starts on the day of Kartik Shukla Chaturthi and ends on Saptami.

-This festival is celebrated for worshipping the sun god 'Suryadev'.

Places for celebrating Chhath

-As Janakpur is also called the city of ponds, Chhath is celebrated in almost all ponds of Janakpur like 'Dasarath Talau', 'Gangasagar', 'Janaki Sarobar', 'Gordhoi', 'Agnikund', Angraj Sar', 'Dhanushsagar', etc. which are decorated by youth clubs with tent and pandal (a shelter erected with upright poles having roofs of bamboo matting, generally in Nepal and India). The main place for the Chhath celebration is the 'Madhesh area' (Terai community of Nepal. However, nowadays it is also spread to the other parts of Nepal like Hetauda, Pokhara, and Kathmandu. Not only this, Chhath is also celebrated in various parts of Narayani zone like Tadi, Parsa, Padampur and Madi.

-Surya Pratima (Statue of the sun god) and 'Akhand deep' (diyo) is kept near the ponds and rivers. Akhanda dip (the diyo which should be burnt continuously during the worship) and statue (Pratima) of the sun god are made at the banks of various rivers and ponds.

The 4 Days of Chhath

Day 1:
The first day of Chhath is called 'Nahay Khay' which occurs on 'Chaturthi'. On this day, the people who take chhath brat (fasting) take a bath for being sacred and eat 'Arwa-arwain' (the sacred food of chhath cooked on a soil stove, eaten only once on that day). They also eat only vegetarian food and wear pure clothes (mainly new saree of turmeric colour).

Day 2:
-On the day of Panchami, they take fast for the whole day. On this evening, they eat khir (rice pudding) cooked on the earthen stove (chulho) and earthen pot. The rice is called 'arwa chamla'. This pudding is made using sakkhar (Veli). It is offered to various gods and goddesses in the form of Prasad and then eaten by the one who takes fast as well as their family members. This day is also called 'kharna'.

Day 3:
-On the evening of Khasthi, the god is offered 'Argha', known as 'Sajhuka Arghya' in Maithili. It is the word for different kinds of offerings like banana, orange, supari (beetle nut), diyo, dhup (a kind of dust of dhupi wood which gives a good smell when burnt), agarbatti (incense sticks). lemon, singar (cosmetic items for chhathi mata),

singhara (a kind of purple fruit found in water (in the shape of samosa), sugarcane, thakuwa (a kind of bread made from wheat flour and veli- a brown sweet), bhushwa (round balls made of rice flour with veli), coconut, etc. these things are put in nanglo (a kind of round plate made of bamboo), kansupti (a sort of square plate made of bamboo for putting various things), dhakna (earthen bowl-larger), and sarwa (earthen bowl-smaller).

-Other things offered to the sun god are dhaki (for keeping things), dagri (for winnowing cereals), of bamboo and statues of kosiya-kurbar as well as an elephant made using soil.

-While giving argha, the people tell their wishes to the sun god and request for their fulfilment. This day is also called 'sajhiya ghate'. They also pray for the long life, well-being, and good health of their family members. At this time, they worship the setting sun.

-Those who don't take fast take the things for argha in the 'chhath ghat' (tent made around the ponds during chhath).

Day 4:

-In the morning of Saptami, they take bath and take the required things with the help of male family members to the chhath ghat and worship in shirshopta. They worship the rising sun and end this festival. This day is also called 'bihanaiya' or 'bhoreghat' in Bhojpuri.

-When they return home, they worship well and cow. They also take blessings from the elders and give their blessings to their younger ones. After that, they eat ginger, sweets, and hot water, to break their fasting.

-They usually take a fast of 48 hours on the day of giving 'argha' without taking even water ('nirjala brat').

Sama Chakewa

Sama Chakewa

-It is a festival symbolizing the love between sister and brother in Mithila.

-This festival is generally celebrated in the different districts of Terai like Sarlahi, Mahottari, Siraha, Saptari, Parsa, and Bara.

-It starts on the day of Kartik Shukla Panchami and continues for ten days. On this day, girls collect soil from the river to make idols.

-During these 10 days, they sing songs in a group while playing 'Sama Chakewa' for their brother's long life. The girls and women play 'Sama Chakewa' for the long life of their brother. They put the idols of chakewa & sama in a basket and meet near chhath ghats, singing various songs.

-On the day of Ekadashi ('Dev Uthan Ekadashi'), they decorate the idols with different colours and pieces of jewellery. It is done with the belief of making sama, the bride and preparing her to go to her groom's house.

-On the last day of sama chakewa (Kartik Purnima), the girls dive into the river and immerse the idols there. This day symbolizes the day of sending 'sama' to her groom's house. On this day, sisters fill the hands of their brothers with their favourite things. The main things offered are beaten rice, thakuwa, and bhuswa in a handkerchief. Also, they provide other things which their brothers like their favourite chocolates and other things. This is called 'faar varnai' in Maithili.

-Those who don't have their brother or sister celebrate this festival with the brother and sister in their neighbourhood.

-Song sung on the last day of Sama Chakewa

'Sam chako sam chako aiha he aiha he

Jotla khet me bhasiha he bhasiha he

Sab rang patiya ochhabiha he ochhabiha he

Oi patiya par kayo jana kayo jana

Chhote bade sayo jana sayo jana…..'

-Meaning: 'Sama chakewa, keep on coming. We'll put worship you and give you farewell. We all will sit on the mats in groups of a hundred……'

Other Events in Tihar

Laxmi Jhaki

-Shown in Kapilvastu (mainly in Taulihawa, Barrohiya, Bahadurgunj, Lawani, Mahrajgunj, Krishnanagar, and Chandrauta).

-More than 50 jhaki are shown in these places.

-Crowd of people showing jhaki is seen in the morning, evening, and night.

-the whole area is decorating with the blinking lights along with the sound is religious songs as well as vajan and kirtan (songs sung to please the goddess) making the environment very intersting.

-It generally begins on the day of Laxmi Puja and is continued.

-On the next day of vaitika, the jhaki is taken to the river and lake for bisarjan (ending) with proper rituals.

Sorathi Dance

-A famous dance presented in Tihar by mostly Magar and Gurung communities.

-Mostly seen in Tamankhola, Badigad, Galkot, and Nisikhola areas of Baglung.

-It begins one week before Tihar.

-In this dance, a male is dressed in the form of a female. He is called 'Singauru'.

-In teams, some old people play 'madal' (a Nepali folk musical instrument) and sing songs.

-Other people too sing and dance with them.

-Before a decade, Sorathi dance was seen mostly in the western villages of Baglung.

-Nowadays, as the youths are losing interest in learning these kinds of traditional dances and songs, this dance is becoming rare.

Hurra Dance

-Famous in Solukhumbu.

-Also shown in other parts of Nepal like Tapting, Fatanje, Kerung, Tamakhani, Kharikhola, and Waksakhani.

-Performed by the 'Magar community' for preserving the language and culture of the local people.

-They make groups and peform singing as well as dancing in their cultural dresses.

-Favoured by tourists.

-Becoming rare nowadays.

Naming of Tihar

Why the name 'Swati Nakha'?

-It's a name given by Newar for Tihar, probably due to one of these 3 assumptions:

(i) As Gaitihar falls on Swati Nakshatra on the day of Aunsi.

(ii) It is a word for 'Tihar' in the Newari language.

(iii) As Tihar is celebrated for mainly 3 days-Laxmi Puja, Mha Puja, and Vai Tika, hence 'Swanti' means the festival of 3 days.

Why the name 'Dipawali'?

-People light diyos in the various corners of their houses like gates, windows, doors, roofs, etc. in clay items or banana sutla or leaves' khori which creates twinkles for 3 days starting from Laxmi puja to Vai Tika.

Why the name 'Yamapanchak'?

-It is said that once, Dharmaraj took a leave from his daily work for some days and went to meet his sister Jamuna. thus, this festival is celebrated to memorize the love between Jamuna and Dharamaraj.

Introduction

Tihar

-Celebrated in the Autumn season.

-Also symbolizes a Festival of Seven Colors' or 'Brightness of diyo-batti' or 'music of deusi-vailo'or 'the smell of selroti' or the festival of 'rangoli'.

-Some people start Tihar from the day of Kartik Krishna Dwadashi by worshipping Lord Ganesh but practically, it starts from the day of Kartik Krishna Trayodashi.

-Some people also put ghee or oil in the khori (bin) made of leaves or banana fibre (kera ko sutla) for light.

-In the old days, miniature candles were used instead of blinking light bulbs ('jhilimili batti').

-One month before Tihar, the markets of Nepal are filled with spices, things for worship, and decorating materials.

-The garlands of marigolds and other flowers are sold in Tihar.

-The clay items like Kalash, diyo, etc. are seen in the markets during this festival.

-Starts on Kartik Krishna Trayodashi and ends on Kartik Shukla Dwitiya.

-It is also known as the 'Yamapanchak parwa'.

-As paddy was the source of income in ancient times, hence, Goddess Laxmi was worshipped in Kartik. it's because the season of cutting paddy is generally in Kartik.